Countries of the World

Robert Anderson

Michael Dunford and Francesco Pastore, Consultants

NATIONAL GEOGRAPHIC

WASHINGTON, D.C.

Contents

taly's location on the Mediterranean linked it with the trade routes of the ancient civilizations that developed in the region. With the city of Rome's rise to power, the Italian peninsula became the center of a huge empire that lasted for centuries. Since then Italian art, architecture, and culture have had a worldwide influence. Italy is also at the heart of the Catholic Church, which is governed from the Vatican City in Rome.

UNESCO, the cultural body of the United Nations, puts Italy at the top of its cultural heritage list because of the country's historical and artistic treasures. Italy also has many areas of outstanding natural wonders. Italians are proud to live in what they boast is *the* country of art and beauty.

Italy has not only played a key role in Europe's history, but also plays an important role in modern international politics. It was one of the founders of the European Union and is a member of the Group of Eight (G8), a forum for eight of the world's most powerful nations.

Despite recent changes in Italians' habits and outlook, Italian society is still fairly traditional. The teachings of the Catholic Church exert a strong influence on everyday life and a low percentage of women work outside the home, mainly because they are involved in caring for children and the elderly. The household remains the center of social life. Over 90 percent of young people age 24 or under and 83 percent of those age 30 or under still live with their parents.

There has always been a big economic gap between the North and the South, which includes Sicily and Sardinia. This difference affects every aspect of life, including welfare, safety, education, employment, and health care. The South has no natural resources, such as coal, and its

land is mountainous, making most of it unsuitable for farming. While industry developed in the North, the South remained poor. Although the economic gap is narrowing, the issue is still an important one for Italy's policymakers.

This book will introduce you to Italy's geography, environment, history, culture, politics, and economy. A thriving economy, natural and cultural wealth, and some of the best food in the world combine to give most Italians an enviable quality of life and enormous pride in their country.

▲ This artist painting a street scene in the village of **Portofino** is part of Italy's rich artistic tradition.

Francesco Pastore

Francesco Pastore, Ph.D.
Assistant Professor of Economics
Seconda Università di Napoli

Countries of the World: Italy

Seas
and
Mountains

O N SUNNY DAYS in late spring, Italians ski high on Mont Blanc, on the border with France. Most Italians live close to one of Italy's two towering mountain ranges, the Alps and the Apennines, and skiing is very popular. Italian skiing gear is nearly as fashionable as the clothes people wear to work or to school. Some people buy new outfits for skiing every year.

Yet, just 175 miles (280 km) from Mont Blanc, locals and tourists alike enjoy the sandy beaches and warm waters of resorts like Levanto. Many Italian families return to the same beach resort year after year for their summer vacations. In the evening, beachgoers relax over long meals in busy outdoor restaurants and chat late into the night.

◄ The fishing village of Vernazza clings to the cliffs above the Ligurian Sea. Its castle was built in the 1500s to protect the inhabitants from pirates.

WHAT'S THE WEATHER LIKE?

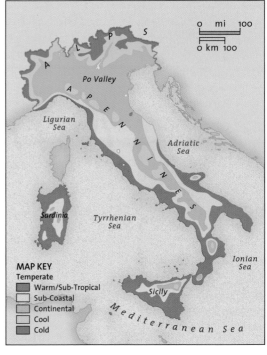

Most of Italy has a temperate climate, with warm, dry summers and mild winters. Occasionally a warm, humid wind named the sirocco blows from North Africa. It brings higher temperatures than usual. Rainfall is heaviest in the north, near the Alps and the Val Padana. There is less rain in the south and on the islands of Sicily and Sardinia. The map opposite shows the physical features of Italy. Labels on this map and on similar maps throughout this book identify places pictured in each chapter.

Average Temperature & Rainfall

Average High/Low Temperatures; Yearly Rainfall

Bolzano (Alps)
73° F (22° C) / 33° F (0° C); 28 in (70 cm)

Milan (Val Padana)
74° F (23° C) / 34° F (1° C); 42 in (108 cm)

Florence (Central Italy)
75° F (24° C) / 41° F (5° C); 36 in (91 cm)

Taranto (Southern Italy)
78° F (25° C) / 48° F (9° C); 17 in (43 cm)

Palermo (Sicily)
80° F (27° C) / 54° F (12° C); 18 in (48 cm)

Cagliari (Sardinia)
75° F (24° C) /49° F (9° C); 19 in (50cm)

Fast Facts

> **OFFICIAL NAME:** Italian Republic
> **FORM OF GOVERNMENT:** republic
> **CAPITAL:** Rome
> **POPULATION:** 58,093,000
> **OFFICIAL LANGUAGE:** Italian
> **MONETARY UNIT:** Euro
> **AREA:** 116,324 square miles (301,277 square kilometers)
> **BORDERING NATIONS:** France, Switzerland, Austria, Slovenia, San Marino, Vatican City
> **HIGHEST POINT:** Mont Blanc de Courmayeur, 15,577 feet (4,748 meters)
> **LOWEST POINT:** Mediterranean Sea, 0 feet (0 meters)
> **MAJOR MOUNTAIN RANGES:** Alps, Apennines
> **MAJOR RIVERS:** Po, Adige, Arno, Tiber

Mont Blanc
de Courmayeur
(Highest point in Italy)
15,577 ft
4,748 m

SWITZERLAND

AUSTRIA

Bolzano

A   L   P   S

Dolomites

VENICE,
page 10

SLOVENIA

Lake
Como

Lake
Garda

Venice

FRANCE

Milan

Po

Po Valley

Adige

Po

Gulf of
Venice

CROATIA

ITALY   Europe

Atlantic
Ocean

Africa

A
P
E
N
N
I
N
E
S

PORTOFINO,
page 5

Portofino
Levanto
Vernazza

Gulf of
Genoa

VERNAZZA,
pages 2, 6

TUSCAN
LANDSCAPE,
page 1

Florence

Arno

MONACO

Ligurian Sea

Siena

Elba

Corsica
(FRANCE)

Strait of Bonifacio

FISHERMEN,
page 15

Sardinia

Cagliari

PO DELTA,
page 11

SAN MARINO

Adriatic
Sea

Gran Sasso d'Italia

Tiber

VATICAN CITY

Rome

Vesuvius
4,203 ft
1,281 m

Naples
Pompeii

Sant'Angelo

EARTHQUAKE,
page 13

Tyrrhenian
Sea

BOSNIA AND
HERZEGOVINA

MONTENEGRO

Promontorio
del Gargano

FIGS,
page 13

Taranto

Gulf of
Taranto

Strait of Otranto

Ionian
Sea

miles   100

km   100

MAP KEY

National capital

Selected city

Elevation

Ancient Roman site

Lipari
Islands

Stromboli

MOUNT ETNA,
page 14

Cape San Vito

Palermo

Sicily

Strait of Messina

Etna
10,867 ft
3,315 m

SICILIAN WALL LIZARD,
page 12

Strait of Sicily

Pantelleria

M e d i t e r r a n e a n   S e a

MALTA

Pelagian
Islands

Physical Map

VENICE: THE CITY BUILT ON THE SEA

Venice is one of the world's most beautiful and unusual cities. Its palaces and churches stand not on regular streets but on canals, and many people move around by boat. The city was founded over 1,400 years ago on a collection of muddy islands in a wide, shallow lagoon. Over the years, trade helped make Venice one of the most powerful cities in Europe. It built an empire that covered large parts of Italy. Today hundreds of thousands of tourists visit the city every year.

Venice, though, is under threat. It has been sinking into the mud for centuries. Today, rising sea levels cause frequent floods. During very high tides Venetians have to cross their squares on raised wooden walkways (right). In 2003 workers began installing barriers between the lagoon around Venice and the sea. The barriers will be raised when very high tides are due, protecting the city from the flood waters.

Shaping the Land

The mountains and the sea have shaped Italy. The seas around the 4,700-mile (7,600-km) coast have provided food and carried the trade that made Italy wealthy. The seas have brought travelers with new ideas to Italy and carried away Italians emigrating to find a new life.

Mountain ranges crisscross the country, dividing it into regions. Each region has developed its own traditions, dialects, and foods. Many Italians are proud of the differences that make their region special and boast that their food is the best in Italy. The mountains also isolate Italy from other countries. The Alps cut across the top of Italy. They form a natural defense for the country that is far better than any wall.

The Alps contain hundreds of "rivers" of ice that formed millions of years ago. These glaciers once pushed down over the plains, but when temperatures rose in the last 10,000 years, the glaciers retreated. They left behind a series of long, thin lakes that look like a necklace when seen from above. The lakes are lined with beautiful villages and are a popular destination for tourists.

Val Padana: The Prosperous North

The Alpine foothills give way to the large plain of the Val Padana, which is crossed by the mighty Po River. At 405 miles (652 km), the Po is by far Italy's longest river and its only navigable one. Where the Po flows into the sea, it forms a marshy delta.

For centuries the Po has been a blessing to farmers. They use its waters to irrigate vast patchworks of fertile fields. Today farmers grow wheat, sugar beets, rice, and corn.

▼ **The Po Delta is so peaceful and remote that people built monasteries and churches there to follow their religion without distractions.**

The Val Padana is home to some of Italy's largest cities, as well as to much of its industry. The Italians are taking steps to ensure that the cities and industries of the North do not pollute the waters of the Po or the skies above the plain.

Italy's Backbone

From the western end of the Alps, the Apennines stretch some 870 miles (1,400 km) down the entire peninsula. They are much smaller than the Alps, but snow still lies on the higher peaks year-round.

The wooded hills west of the mountains are home to many of Italy's historic cities, including Florence, Siena, and the capital, Rome. It was in these central regions that the ancient Etruscans and Romans developed some of Europe's first great civilizations, more than two and a half thousand years ago. The Romans built a network of superb, straight, paved roads that led out of Rome in every direction. Circular columns marked distances. The roads enabled Rome's armies to move quickly and played a major part in the expansion of the Roman Empire. Many of the roads have survived and can still be seen today.

▶ In the Mezzogiorno lizards, such as this Sicilian Wall Lizard, are a common sight sunning themselves on rocks or on the walls of homes. They dart into crevices when they are alarmed.

Mezzogiorno: The Midday Land

The south of Italy boasts spectacular stretches of coast and ancient sites such as the Roman towns of Pompeii and Herculaneum. Naples, its principal city, sprawls around the edge of a sweeping bay. The summer sun is so fierce that the whole region south of Abruzzi and Molise has become known as the Mezzogiorno (meht-soh-JOR-noh)—the Italian word for midday.

▲ Figs are a traditional crop in the south.

▼ Italians suffer more earthquakes than any other Europeans. The 1980 earthquake brought death and destruction to many towns, such as Sant' Angelo.

The vegetation is mainly dry shrubland that the Italians call the *macchia*, which means "thicket." There are very few rivers, and some towns rely on water carried by aqueducts from wetter regions nearby. Some of the water channels were built by the Romans two thousand years ago.

On the "heel" of Italy, in contrast, there are extensive plains. Farmers use this valuable fertile land to grow hardy crops such as olives, almonds, and figs.

An Unstable Landscape

Italians have become accustomed to living in a geologically active country, with earthquakes, floods, landslides, and volcanoes. Every year there are many minor earth tremors, but some are far more serious. In 1980 an earthquake

A DYNAMIC TRIO: ITALY'S ACTIVE VOLCANOES

No other country in Europe has as many volcanoes as Italy. The Italian peninsula stands on a fault line—a deep fracture in the Earth's surface that has created volcanoes and produces frequent earthquakes. In A.D. 79 Mount Vesuvius erupted near Naples. Ash from the volcano buried the ancient Roman cities of Pompeii and Herculaneum and killed many thousands of people. Its last major eruption was in 1631, but volcano experts warn that a new eruption would destroy everything within a four mile (7-km) range. Mount Etna on Sicily (below) is one of the world's most active volcanoes. Stromboli is one of the few volcanoes that display continuous activity.

▲ Molten lava forces its way through rocks, building up pressure until it produces a vast explosion and widespread destruction.

Ligurian Sea

ALPS

ITALY

Adriatic Sea

Rome ✪

Sardinia

Tyrrhenian Sea

Vesuvius
4,203 ft
1,281 m

Stromboli
3,031 ft
924 m

Ionian Sea

Sicily ▲ Etna
10,867 ft
3,315 m

Mediterranean Sea

0   mi   100
0   km   100

MAP KEY
△ Selected volcano

near Naples killed more than two and a half thousand people. Three volcanoes—Etna, Stromboli, and Vesuvius—have erupted in the last hundred years.

Italy's Islands

Mountains also dominate Italy's two major islands, Sicily and Sardinia. Sicily, the largest island in the Mediterranean, is divided from the "toe" of the mainland only by the narrow waterway called the Strait of Messina. Close to Africa, the three Pelagian Islands form Italy's most southern territory.

Sardinian villages are famous for their "witches." They make potions for local people who seek their help for sickness or other problems. The witches are usually women. They use a language known only on the island to pass on their secrets to their daughters.

▼ Sardinian fishermen sort their catch. Fish and shellfish are big business around Italy's coast and on the islands—and make for a tasty diet.

Humans
and
Nature

FOR TWENTY-TWO CENTURIES, Italians and their ancestors have cleared fields, grazed livestock—and hunted wild animals. Much of the country has been shaped by human habitation. The forests that once covered large areas have been cut down. The plains and the coasts are covered with crops and vineyards. Tall poplar trees stand amid the fields like exclamation marks.

In Italy's remote wild places and its many national parks, however, animals such as the brown bear can still enjoy wilderness largely untouched by humans. Italy's protected environments range from Sila Grande's deep lakes and stands of tall pines, some of which are over 500 years old, to the marshy wetlands of the Gargano with its flocks of migratory birds.

◀ **The powerful Eurasian brown bear lives a solitary life except when mating or when a mother is raising her cubs.**

PROTECTED PARADISES

The best places to see Italy's wildlife are its 21 national parks. They cover 5 percent of the country's area and include mountains, highlands, coastal areas, and Mediterranean islands. Gran Paradiso became Italy's first national park in 1922, having been set up as a royal reserve in 1856 to protect the ibex, a wild goat.

The map opposite shows vegetation zones—what grows where—in Italy. Vegetation zones form ecosystems, environments that support specific plant and animal life. Italy is home to some of Europe's last populations of wild mammals such as wolves and the goatlike chamois.

▲ The Eurasian otter is perfectly adapted to its aquatic life with webbed toes, a powerful rudderlike tail, ears and nostrils that close while underwater, and a double layer of fur that is both warm and waterproof.

Species at Risk

Italy's dwindling natural habitats, as well as intensive hunting, have led to the extinction of many native creatures in recent centuries. In the 20th century alone, 13 species of animals and birds were lost.

The species on the right are among those at risk.

> Mediterranean monk seal
> Northern right whale
> Fin whale
> Eurasian otter
> Bechstein's bat
> Geoffroy's bat
> Lesser horseshoe bat
> Long-fingered bat
> Mediterranean horseshoe bat
> Western barbastelle (bat)
> Mehely's horseshoe bat

> Garden dormouse
> Mouflon (sheep)
> Wild goat
> Sardinian cave salamander
> Audouin's gull
> Corncrake (bird)
> Ferruginous pochard (duck)
> Lesser kestrel
> Greater spotted owl
> Slender-billed curlew
> White-headed duck

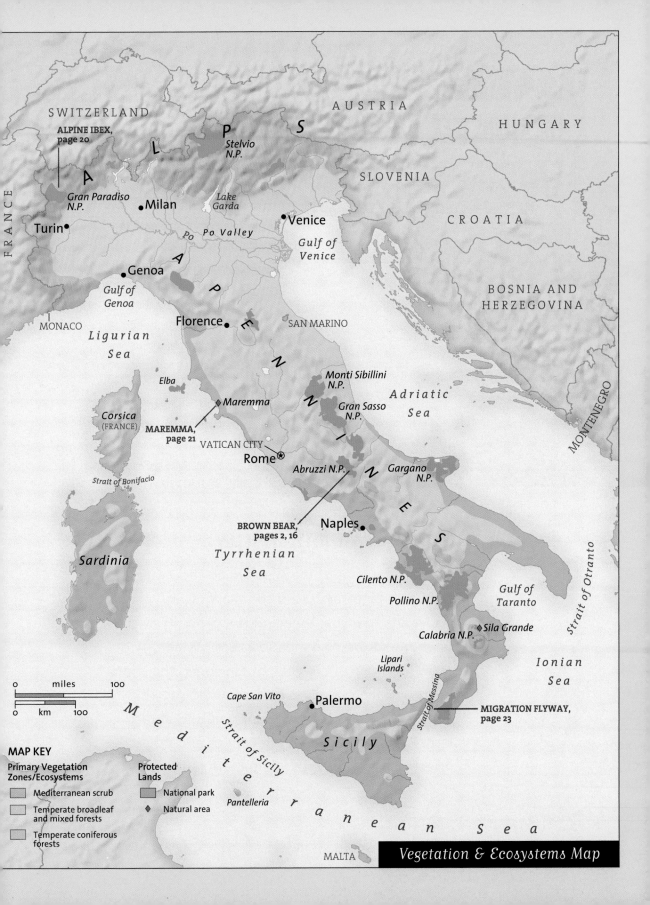

SWITZERLAND

ALPINE IBEX,
page 20

*Stelvio
N.P.*

A L P S

AUSTRIA

HUNGARY

SLOVENIA

CROATIA

FRANCE

*Gran Paradiso
N.P.*

●Milan

*Lake
Garda*

●Venice

*Gulf of
Venice*

BOSNIA AND
HERZEGOVINA

Turin●

Po

Po Valley

●Genoa

*Gulf of
Genoa*

A
P
E

MONACO

*Ligurian
Sea*

Florence●

SAN MARINO

*Adriatic
Sea*

MONTENEGRO

Elba

N

◆*Maremma*

*Monti Sibillini
N.P.*

Corsica
(FRANCE)

MAREMMA,
page 21

VATICAN CITY

*Gran Sasso
N.P.*

N

Strait of Bonifacio

Rome⊛

Abruzzi N.P.

*Gargano
N.P.*

I

BROWN BEAR,
pages 2, 16

Naples●

*Tyrrhenian
Sea*

N

E

Sardinia

Cilento N.P.

S

Pollino N.P.

*Gulf of
Taranto*

*Ionian
Sea*

Strait of Otranto

Calabria N.P.   ◆*Sila Grande*

*Lipari
Islands*

Strait of Messina

0   miles   100

0   km   100

Cape San Vito

Palermo●

MIGRATION FLYWAY,
page 23

*M
e
d
i
t*

Strait of Sicily

S i c i l y

MAP KEY

**Primary Vegetation
Zones/Ecosystems**

**Protected
Lands**

Mediterranean scrub

National park

Pantelleria

Temperate broadleaf
and mixed forests

◆ Natural area

Temperate coniferous
forests

*e
r
r
a
n
e
a
n   S e a*

MALTA

Vegetation & Ecosystems Map

THE ALPINE IBEX

Walkers high in the Alps may be lucky enough to spot one of Italy's most spectacular animals—the Alpine ibex (below). A type of wild goat, the ibex is easy to identify by its sword-shaped, knobby horns. Males grow horns up to 34 inches (85 cm) long. Ibex graze on plants and moss near the snowline, where there are few competitors for food. Their sturdy forelegs and tough hooves make them sure-footed climbers on steep cliffs.

The ibex was once common, but it was nearly extinct by the 18th century. People hunted it for its horns, which were used in traditional cures. New herds were created in the Gran Paradiso National Park. Careful conservation means that today there are about 30,000 ibex in the Alps.

Wonders of the Alps

The lower slopes of the Alps are covered with forests of beech, pine, larch, and spruce. If hikers venture above the tree line, they find low-growing shrubs and open meadows. The meadows are covered by deep snow for much of the year, but in spring the snow melts and the grassland bursts into flower. The flowers have large and brilliant petals to attract insects, because there are few bees and other insects to carry pollen to help them reproduce.

Alpine flowers have adapted to protect themselves from the cold. Some have dark buds that absorb warmth from the sun, while others have thin coverings of woolly hair.

The Fragrant Thicket

The rocky, warm south of Italy and the island of Sardinia are home to the *macchia*, that are made up of shrubs that like dry conditions, including sage, gorse, and juniper. The shrubs grow 7 feet (2 m) tall and have spikes or leathery leaves that do not allow much water to evaporate. The thorny *macchia* can be a formidable barrier to larger animals—and people. After the winter rains, the *macchia* bursts into radiant bloom. Orchids, gladioli, and irises flower beneath the

▲ **A baby wild boar basks in the sunshine.**

▼ **Like much of Italy, the coastal area known as the Maremma has been shaped by people. In the past, the marshes that gave the area its name helped prevent its development.**

▲ The male cicada makes the loudest sound in the insect world as it calls for a mate.

▼ Juniper berries can take three years to ripen. For centuries people have used the berries to add flavor to game dishes, as well as for medicinal purposes.

shrubs. The air becomes fragrant with wild herbs, such as rosemary, lavender, and thyme.

Farther south, the soil is rockier and drier. The plants that grow here are sticklike shrubs. This kind of cover is called *garrigue*, or *gariga*. It does not support many large animals, but reptiles, including geckos and snakes, bask in the warm sun. The many insects include the cicada, whose rasping call is an almost constant soundtrack in the summer.

Dangers and Threats

Every year millions of birds visit Italy as they fly to Africa to escape the cold winters of northern Europe. Their route takes them across the Mediterranean Sea. Many fly down the Italian peninsula so they can stay near sources of food and fresh water. Their route brings them into danger from hunters, who trap or shoot even small birds for sport, to eat as a delicacy, or to cage and sell as pets.

The complex relationship between Italians and nature continues. In the decades after World War II (1939–45), industrial development made pollution a serious problem in the north. Sprawling towns, resorts, and other tourist developments contributed to coastal erosion. Forest fires were on the increase, especially during the hot, dry summers. But, by the end of the 20th century, the Italians had introduced new laws to reduce pollution. They also created new national parks, where natural environments and environments shaped by humans both play an important role in protecting Italy's wealth of animals and plants.

▲ The Strait of Messina is one of the most important flyways for Montagu's Harrier, a long-winged bird of prey. The harrier breeds on lowland plains in temperate parts of Europe and Russia and then migrates to Africa, where it spends the winter.

From
Empire
to
Republic

N THE FIFTEENTH CENTURY, the city of Florence in Tuscany drew artists and architects from all over Italy. Its powerful princes commissioned palaces and churches from leading architects. There was plenty of work for painters and sculptors, who decorated the new buildings. Today, the same buildings draw tourists from around the world.

By the time Florence reached the height of its power, Italy already had a rich history. There are reminders everywhere of its long past. On the island of Sardinia stand thousands of cone-shaped stone towers known as nuraghi. They date from about 1500 B.C. The builders were among the oldest of the many cultures that have flourished across Italy.

◄ **The Arno River runs through the center of Florence, which is dominated by the dome of its duomo (cathedral) at right.**

EARLY CULTURES

The first developed societies emerged in Italy in about 1200 B.C. The Ligurians moved into the peninsula from what is now southern France. Another people, the Italics, arrived from Central Europe. About four centuries later, colonists from Greece began to settle in southern Italy and Sicily.

At the same time, a new people emerged in central Italy. Historians are not sure where the Etruscans came from, but by the sixth century B.C. they had created Etruria, a group of states based around walled cities. They grew rich on sea trade. To the south of Etruria, Latin and Sabine peoples lived in villages on hills near the Tiber River. In the early sixth century B.C., the villages merged to create a settlement named Rome, which became a strong city-state.

Originally the state was ruled by a king, but in 509 B.C. it became a republic. The Romans conquered the Etruscan town of Veii in 396 B.C. and, over the next hundred years, took over the whole peninsula. From there, they set out to build a vast empire.

▲ An Etruscan plowman guides a team of yoked oxen in this bronze group dating from the fourth century B.C.

Time line

This chart shows the approximate dates for major societies that developed in Italy between 1200 B.C. and A.D. 500.

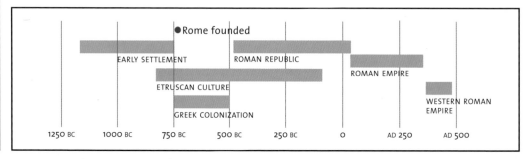

● Rome founded

EARLY SETTLEMENT

ROMAN REPUBLIC

ROMAN EMPIRE

ETRUSCAN CULTURE

GREEK COLONIZATION

WESTERN ROMAN EMPIRE

1250 BC   1000 BC   750 BC   500 BC   250 BC   0   AD 250   AD 500

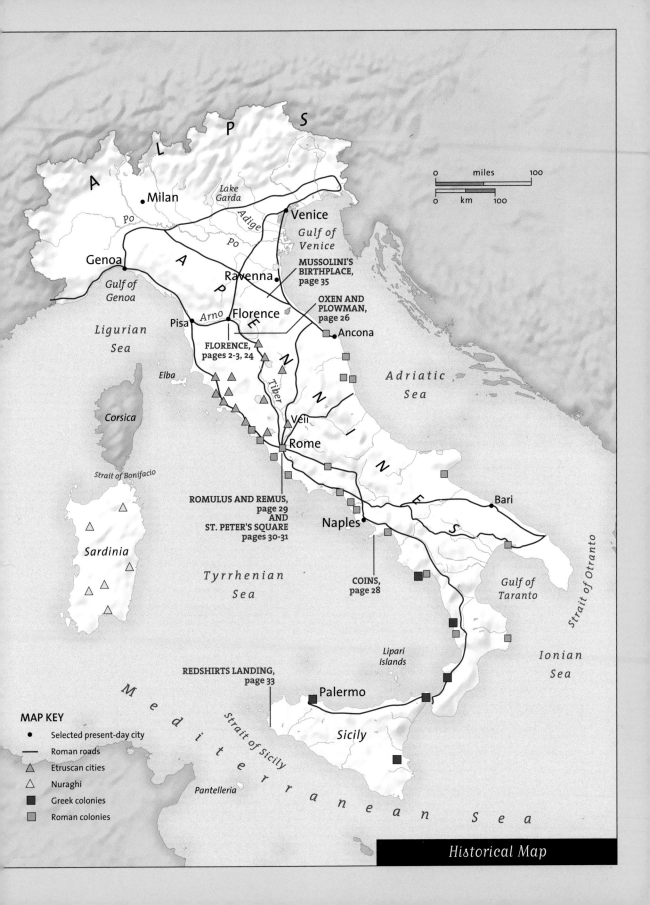

A
L
P
S

• Milan

Lake Garda

Po

Adige

Po

Venice

Gulf of Venice

Ravenna •

MUSSOLINI'S BIRTHPLACE, page 35

OXEN AND PLOWMAN, page 26

Genoa

Gulf of Genoa

A
P
E

Pisa • *Arno* Florence

FLORENCE, pages 2-3, 24

Ancona ■

Ligurian Sea

Elba

Tiber

N

Adriatic Sea

Veii •

Rome

Corsica

Strait of Bonifacio

ROMULUS AND REMUS, page 29 AND ST. PETER'S SQUARE pages 30-31

N

Sardinia

Bari •

N

Naples •

COINS, page 28

Tyrrhenian Sea

E

S

Gulf of Taranto

Strait of Otranto

REDSHIRTS LANDING, page 33

Lipari Islands

Ionian Sea

Palermo •

Sicily

M e d i t e r r a n e a n

Strait of Sicily

Pantelleria

S e a

MAP KEY

• Selected present-day city

— Roman roads

△ Etruscan cities

△ Nuraghi

■ Greek colonies

■ Roman colonies

miles
0 — 100

km
0 — 100

Historical Map

Greeks, Etruscans, and Latins

From the middle of the eighth century B.C., ancient Greeks began to found cities on the coasts of Sicily and southern Italy. The new colonists brought ideas and culture from their homeland, only 60 miles (100 km) across the Ionian Sea. They mixed with the Bronze Age peoples who already inhabited Italy, such as the Italics and the Ligurians. A distinctive culture emerged that was famed for its poets, painters, and sculptors.

The Greeks were not the only city-builders in Italy. In central Italy, the Etruscans were developing the first great Italian civilization. By the seventh century their

▲ The Romans used gold and silver coins for official purposes and brass and bronze coins for everyday transactions.

THE ROMAN EMPIRE

From Rome, the Romans spread to conquer first the whole of Italy and then a vast empire. At its greatest extent, in A.D. 117, the Roman Empire stretched from Portugal in the west to Syria in the east, and from Britain in the north to the North African deserts. It covered some

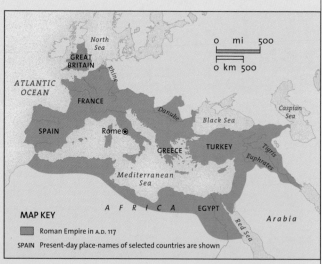

MAP KEY

▪ Roman Empire in A.D. 117

SPAIN Present-day place-names of selected countries are shown

2.3 million square miles (5.9 million sq. km)—roughly two-thirds the size of the United States—and had an estimated population of 120 million people. The empire was divided into provinces, one of which was Italia (Italy) itself. Other important cities in Roman Italy included Mediolanum (Milan), Florentia (Florence), and Ravenna.

homeland, Etruria, had flourishing cities. Etruscan ships dominated the Mediterranean trading routes.

One of the oldest cities of central Italy was Rome, in the region of Latium. Its early inhabitants were known as Latins. For a time Rome was ruled by the Etruscans, but in 510 B.C. the Latins threw out the king and made Rome an independent republic the following year.

Rome Builds an Empire

The Romans soon increased their territory. They were skilled warriors, and by 218 B.C. they ruled virtually all of the Italian peninsula. Roman culture and the Latin language spread almost everywhere. They helped shape Italy's language and culture. Important cities like Rome and Florence were connected by a network of well-made roads. Aqueducts carried water into the cities, where the citizens enjoyed bathing in great public bathhouses.

The Romans built a huge empire that stretched over much of Europe and into West Asia and North

▲ According to legend Rome was founded by twin brothers, Romulus and Remus, who were abandoned as babies. They were found by a she-wolf, who suckled the twins. A shepherd saw the boys with the wolf, took them home, and raised them as his own sons. The twins decided to build a city where they had been found, but they quarreled. Romulus killed Remus and became king of the new city, which was named in his honor.

▲ It has been 1,200 years since the bishop of Rome became known as the pope. Today, the pope is still the head of the Roman Catholic church. Every Easter Sunday, about 100,000 people gather in St. Peter's Square in Rome to receive his blessing.

Africa. Ambitious generals fought to control the mighty empire. In 27 B.C., Octavian became the first sole emperor. He took the name Augustus Caesar.

For more than 400 years, the empire flourished. By the fourth century A.D., however, it was in decline. In 395 the Roman Empire was split in two. The eastern half was ruled from Constantinople (modern Istanbul, Turkey). Called the Byzantine Empire, it would survive for another thousand years.

In 476 Germanic tribes from north of the Alps entered the peninsula and toppled the last emperor of the Western Empire. For centuries, Italy became a network of small states speaking many different languages. Rome's system of laws survived, but much of its learning and culture were lost. The once-great cities were abandoned, and the public baths stood dry and empty.

The Bishop of Rome

One part of Roman life that endured was religion. The emperor Constantine had become a Christian in the early fourth century, and Christianity spread through much of the empire. The bishop of Rome was one of the most powerful of Italy's local rulers and the leader of the Christian church. The Roman bishops took the title pope, or father, and gradually increased both the spiritual and the worldly power of the papacy.

The Renaissance

By the 12th century, the cities of central and northern Italy had recovered from the fall of Rome. They formed states with their surrounding areas, and the city-states grew rich on

ROME: THE ETERNAL CITY

Founded on seven hills on the Tiber River in central Italy, Rome is one of the world's oldest cities. It has been continuously inhabited for some 2,800 years. For about 500 years, it was the capital of the mighty Roman Empire. Since the sixth century it has been almost constantly the seat of one of the world's great religions, Roman Catholicism, and since 1870 it has been the capital of the modern Italian state. Because of its wealth and power, and the rich legacy of its ancient history, the city has been nicknamed the "Eternal City."

City-states

The map shows Italy's city-states in the 15th century. They fought each other for territory. They also competed to have the most awe-inspiring buildings and to employ the best artists, writers, and musicians.

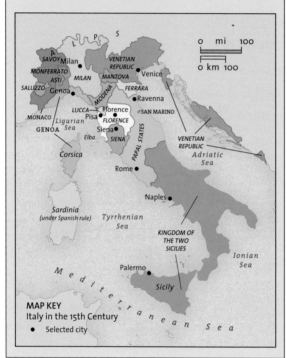

MAP KEY
Italy in the 15th Century
● Selected city

trade. The port of Genoa, for example, controlled much of the spice trade with Asia. The city-states fought among each other to increase their territory. By the mid-15th century, much of Italy was dominated by Milan, Florence, and Venice.

Although Italy could be a violent place, the wealth generated by trade also financed the golden age of culture known as the Renaissance. There was a great blossoming of art and literature, but at the heart of the Renaissance was a set of ideas called humanism. Humanist ideas were based on the works of the ancient Greeks and Romans. They encouraged people to study the world with fresh eyes.

A Country at Last

In the 16th century, the power of the city-states fell sharply. New sea routes to Asia and the Americas drew trade away to countries such as Spain, Britain, and the Netherlands.

In the early 19th century, Italy was still a patchwork of territories. Some regions were ruled by foreign dynasties, including the Spanish Bourbons in the south and the Austrian Habsburgs in the north. Many Italians, however, hoped to create a united country.

In 1859, Victor Emmanuel II, king of Piedmont–Sardinia, and his prime minister, Camillo Cavour, got French help to drive the Austrians out of northern Italy. In 1860 a patriot named Giuseppe Garibaldi led a daring military march to overthrow Bourbon rule in southern Italy. The Kingdom of Italy was proclaimed in 1861, with Victor Emmanuel as its first king.

▲ Giuseppe Garibaldi and a force of 1,000 men, known as the Redshirts, landed in Sicily in 1860. His military victories played a major role in the unification of Italy.

UNIFICATION OF ITALY

In the early 19th century, Italy was a jigsaw of states and territories, but from 1859 to 1870 the Kingdom of Piedmont-Sardinia led the country toward unification. This map shows the routes taken by Garibaldi after his departure from Genoa and King Victor Emmanuel II. It also shows when different parts of Italy became part of the new Kingdom of Italy. The city of Trieste (map p.49) and its surrounding territory did not become part of the unified Italy until the end of World War I (1914–18).

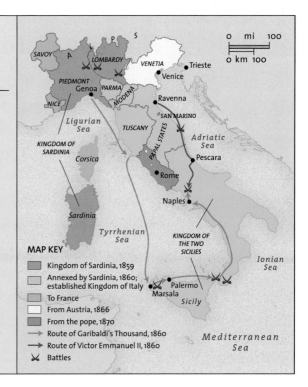

MAP KEY
- Kingdom of Sardinia, 1859
- Annexed by Sardinia, 1860; established Kingdom of Italy
- To France
- From Austria, 1866
- From the pope, 1870
- → Route of Garibaldi's Thousand, 1860
- → Route of Victor Emmanuel II, 1860
- ⚔ Battles

A NEW LIFE

From 1861 to 1985, more than 26 million people left Italy to seek work and a better life in other countries. Many had little education and few possessions and they did not speak the language of their new country. They settled in cramped neighborhoods and worked hard, hoping to make their fortune and then return to Italy. Only one in four came home again.

An Italian family arrives at the immigration center on Ellis Island, New York.

The Rise of Fascism

Cities in the north of the new nation, such as Milan, Turin, and Genoa, quickly developed modern industries. Millions of Italians, especially from the south, moved to the cities to find work. Many others moved abroad.

Italy fought in World War I (1914–18) on the side of Great Britain, France, and the United States. Although the Allies won the war, Italy was left with high prices and unemployment. Many Italians looked to left-wing political parties, such as the communists, to solve the economic crisis. Others looked to Benito Mussolini, founder of the right-wing Fascist Party, who promised to restore prosperity.

In 1922 Mussolini threatened to march his armed followers to Rome to overthrow the government. King Victor Emmanuel III feared that Italy would be torn apart by civil war. He asked Mussolini to be prime minister. Mussolini set up new industries, electrified the railroads, and drained marshy areas. But he also turned Italy into a one-party state, and became its dictator. He suppressed anyone who opposed him.

War and Peace

Mussolini wanted to create a new Roman Empire. In 1935, he invaded the African country of Abyssinia (now Ethiopia). He also made an alliance with the German dictator Adolf Hitler, who shared many of his ideas. The leaders made a further alliance with Japan. In 1940 Mussolini took Italy into World War II (1939–45) on Germany's side against the Allies: Britain, Russia, and later the United States.

In 1943 Allied troops landed in Sicily and fought their way up Italy, helped by Italians who were against Mussolini. The king fired Mussolini and began peace talks. Italian communists captured and executed Mussolini in 1945.

In 1946 the Italians voted to end the monarchy and make Italy a republic again. In 1948 democratic elections were held.

▼ **Benito Mussolini called himself Il Duce (the leader). During the 1920s and 1930s he carried out sweeping reforms that made him highly popular with many Italians.**

Festivals
and
Families

VENICE'S REGATTA is one of Italy's most unusual festivals. The city has celebrated its relationship with the sea in much the same way since the 13th century. Families and visitors line the canals to watch events that have hardly changed in seven hundred years. Crews put on historical costumes for a spectacular parade of old boats on the Grand Canal. Then there are hotly contested rowing races between the city's neighborhoods. At midnight, dramatic fireworks mark the end of an exciting day.

Italy's festivals reflect its many regions, each of which has its own celebrations, foods, and dialects. Most Italians, however, are united by a belief in the importance of the family. Traditionally, they also put the Roman Catholic Church at the heart of daily life.

◀ Crowds line the Grand Canal to watch the colorful ceremonial parade of gondolas and historic craft that takes place in Venice every September.

A DECLINING POPULATION

Italy's population stands at just over 58 million (see map opposite), but it is no longer growing. Italians are having fewer children—perhaps one or two rather than five or more as in the past. Italy's population is also aging, with more than 20 percent over 65 years old, a figure expected to double by 2050. The declining birth rate worries the government as more retired people will have to be supported by fewer young people, and the economy will suffer. They have introduced a bonus for couples having a second child.

▲ Italians celebrate Grandparents' Day on October 2, the feast day of "guardian angels." In many families, it is the grandparents who look after children when their parents are at work.

Common Italian Phrases

Here are a few Italian words and phrases you might use in Italy. Give them a try:

Ciao (CHOW)	Hello/goodbye (informal)
Buon giorno (bwon-JOR-no)	Good morning
Arrivederci (a-ree-ve-DER-chee)	Goodbye
Per favore (per fa-VO-re)	Please
Grazie (GRA-tsye)	Thank you
Prego (PRE-go)	That's fine/What can I do for you?
Mi scusi (me SCU-zi)	Excuse me/ Sorry

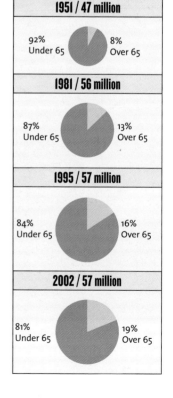

1951 / 47 million
92% Under 65
8% Over 65

1981 / 56 million
87% Under 65
13% Over 65

1995 / 57 million
84% Under 65
16% Over 65

2002 / 57 million
81% Under 65
19% Over 65

Population Map

The Family

The family stands at the heart of Italian society. Families provide support, not only by helping with tasks such as child care but also by helping to find jobs for other family members. Young people often live at home until their 30s, even if they have a job. This is partly because it takes students six or seven years of college to earn a degree. When parents retire, they often go to live with their children. Close-knit families have helped create strong communities.

The family is important to the economy, too. Most businesses—even some very large ones, like the carmaker Fiat—are family run. One bell foundry in the town of Agone in central Italy has been run by the same family for a thousand years.

Family life is changing, however. For one thing, the typical family is becoming smaller. For another, many women

NATIONAL HOLIDAYS

Most public holidays mark religious festivals, but some commemorate key events in Italy's history. Individual towns and cities also have public holidays, usually in honor of their patron saint.

JANUARY 1
New Year's Day
(Capodanno)

JANUARY 6
Epiphany

MARCH/APRIL
Easter Monday (Pasquetta)

APRIL 25
Liberation Day

MAY 1
Labor Day (International
   Worker's Day)

JUNE 2
Republic's Day

AUGUST 15
Feast of the Assumption (Ferragosto)

NOVEMBER 1
All Saints' Day

DECEMBER 8
Feast of the Immaculate Conception

DECEMBER 25
Christmas Day (Natale)

DECEMBER 26
St. Stephen's Day (Santo Stefano)

choose to go to work rather than spend all their time looking after the family.

The Church

Around 97 percent of Italians are Catholics, and on Sunday mornings, towns and cities are filled with the sound of bells calling worshipers to church. The influence of the church is declining, however. Only 35 percent of Italians go to Mass regularly, although the vast majority still get married in church and baptize their children. Many Italians continue to respect the pope but ignore many church teachings, such as its ban on divorce. In recent decades, Islam has become the second largest religion in Italy.

▲ Cardinals from all over the world make up the College of Cardinals, which advises the pope.

▼ In Italy there is a type of coffee for every time and mood.

Varied Regional Foods

Italians seldom eat a sit-down breakfast; they tend to have a cappuccino and a pastry while standing at a counter. Children drink hot chocolate or hot milk rather than coffee. Lunch was once an important meal of three or four

courses, accompanied by wine. As lifestyles change, however, fewer Italians have large lunches. Many families eat their main meal in the evening. Often, they do not sit down until eight o'clock or even later.

Traditional dishes are based on simple ingredients such as fish or vegetables. Recipes are handed down in families for generations. In the South, olive oil and tomatoes are key ingredients; in the North, butter, cheese, and creamy sauces are popular. Pasta, pizza, and a rice dish called risotto are enjoyed everywhere.

▲ Olives are grown throughout Italy. Each region produces a different kind of olive oil with its own distinctive taste. And each region claims that their olive oil is the best!

Celebrating in the Streets

Many towns celebrate Carnevale (car-neh-VAH-lay) in January or February. In the Middle Ages, this was a time of riotous feasts before Lent, the period before

OPERA: A NATIONAL MUSIC

The world's first operas were composed in Italy at the end of the 16th century. Opera reached a height of popularity in the 19th century, when the works of composers like Gioacchino Rossini, Giacomo Puccini, and Giuseppe Verdi were hugely popular. Today opera stars like Luciano Pavarotti are national celebrities, and crowds flock to famous opera houses, such as La Scala (above) in Milan and La Fenice in Venice.

◀ Dozens of towns stage pageants during Holy Week. Participants wear costumes and pâpier-maché masks as they reenact the Easter story.

Easter when Catholics fasted, or ate only a little food. The most famous carnival takes place in Venice, where locals and tourists alike put on elaborate costumes and masks and party in the streets. Easter itself is very solemn. During the nights of Holy Week (Settimana Santa), torch-lit processions wind through the streets re-creating the last hours of Christ's life.

Sports Crazy

Italians are big sports fans, and their main passion is soccer. Two teams dominate the game: Turin's Juventus and AC Milan. Italians are also fans of Formula 1 motor racing, and especially of the team run by the automobile company Ferrari, with its distinctive red cars.

▼ A driver for the Ferrari team prepares for the Monaco Grand Prix. Since Ferrari's first race in 1947, they have had over 5,000 victories on racetracks around the world.

Italy is famous for its sleek sports cars, but Italians also love motorbikes and bicycles. In cities such as Bologna, cycles are a popular form of transportation—as long as it's not too hilly. In winter many people like to take a week's holiday skiing in the Alps.

Arts and Literature

Since the Renaissance (about 1350 through the 1500s), Italy has been renowned for its art and architecture. Its cities are home to many outstanding buildings. In Rome, ancient monuments such as the Colosseum and the Pantheon are joined by Renaissance buildings, such as Michelangelo's beautiful Sforza Chapel built in 1558.

The best-known Italian painters worked during the Renaissance. They include Leonardo da Vinci, Michelangelo, Raphael, and Titian. There have been many other Italian artists, however, including Amedeo Modigliani and Giorgio de Chirico in the 20th century.

Italians have long revered great writers. The national poet is Dante Alighieri, who wrote *The Divine Comedy* in the early 14th century. Dante's long poem imagined a journey through hell and heaven.

▼ Leonardo da Vinci drew this portrait of himself as an old man. He had many talents in addition to his painting. He was also a scientist, engineer, and inventor.

The Movies and TV

The most popular movies in Italy are Hollywood thrillers and action films dubbed into Italian, but Italy also has its own thriving cinema tradition. In the 1950s and 1960s directors such as Federico Fellini, Roberto Rossellini, and Pier Paolo Pasolini made innovative movies that combined realism and fantasy. Movie buffs go to the annual Venice Film Festival, where the *Leone d'Oro* (The Golden Lion) is awarded to the best film.

Italy has numerous television channels, but the state-owned RAI and a company called Fininvest capture about 87 percent of all viewers. When Silvio Berlusconi, whose family owns Fininvest, became prime minister in 1994, he was able to appoint the people to run RAI. Many Italians worried that he could use this power to promote his own political ideas.

SOPHIA LOREN

Glamorous Italian Sophia Loren is a movie icon. She has appeared in more than 100 films and has won an honorary Oscar for lifetime achievement. She was brought up in poverty by her single mother before she won a beauty contest at age 14 and began to take acting classes. Loren later learned English and landed a leading role in a Hollywood movie. She soon became one of the world's most popular actors.

A
Leading
Economy

I N ITALY, POLITICS can often be exciting and noisy. Crowds gather in the streets, even if it's raining, to protest government policies or to show their support for one party or another. Some Italians believe that such public demonstrations are the best way to achieve democracy. But Italy's political parties are sometimes too busy fighting among themselves to tackle the country's problems.

Still, since World War II, Italy has enjoyed an economic transformation. Industry grew, and by the mid-1960s Italy had become one of the world's leading economies. It was a founding member of the European Economic Community, which later became the European Union. In the late 1990s unemployment increased and the government became unpopular.

◄ Under a balloon promoting a labor union, workers gather in Rome during a general strike in 2004 to protest tax cuts that they argued would benefit only the rich.

SELF-RULING REGIONS

Italy is divided into 20 administrative regions, each of which has its own capital, elected council, and government (see political map on the opposite page). Each of the regions, with the exception of tiny Valle d'Aosta, is divided into provinces. The regions and provinces reflect historic identities that come from Renaissance times and before.

All of the regions have a degree of autonomy (self-rule) in local matters. Five regions—Sicily, Trentino-Alto Adige, Valle d'Aosta, Sardinia, and Friuli-Venezia Giulia—where local identity is especially strong, are designated as fully autonomous regions. In recent years—partly in response to political scandals in the 1990s—the central government in Rome has given more powers to the regions. Some Italians, such as members of the Northern League party, want even more local self-rule.

Trading Partners

Italy's principal trading partners are other members of the European Union and the United States. Among its chief exports are textiles, clothing, and shoes, household appliances and furniture, automobiles, and food and wine. Its imports include chemicals, transportation equipment, energy, minerals and metals.

Country	Percent Italy exports
Germany	13.7%
France	12.2%
United States	9.8%
All others combined	64.3%

Country	Percent Italy imports
Germany	17.8%
France	11.3%
Netherlands	5.9%
All others combined	65%

▲ Global brands are everywhere in Italy—but sometimes with a local twist. In Venice, Coca-Cola is delivered not by truck but by red-painted gondolas.

8°E 10°E 12°E 14°E 16°E 18°E 20°E

AUSTRIA

SWITZERLAND

HUNGARY

TRENTINO-ALTO ADIGE

FRIULI-VENEZIA GIULIA

SLOVENIA

46°N

Trento

VALLE D'AOSTA
Aosta

LOMBARDY

VENETO

CROATIA

Brescia
Milan

Verona
Padua

Venice

Trieste

Turin

PIEDMONT

Gulf of Venice

EMILIA-ROMAGNA

Bologna

BOSNIA AND HERZEGOVINA

44°N

Genoa
LIGURIA

SAN MARINO

MONACO

Ligurian Sea

Florence

Urbino

Ancona

TUSCANY

MARCHES

Adriatic Sea

UMBRIA

Elba

Perugia

Corsica (FRANCE)

L'Aquila

42°N

LATIUM

ABRUZZI

MONTENEGRO

VATICAN CITY

Rome

MOLISE

Campobasso

CAMPANIA

Bari

Naples

APULIA

Salerno

Potenza

Taranto

BASILICATA

Tyrrhenian Sea

SARDINIA

Gulf of Taranto

40°N

Cagliari

CALABRIA

Catanzaro

Ionian Sea

miles 100

Lipari Islands

km 100

Palermo

38°N

MAP KEY

SICILY

Catania

⊛ National capital

◉ Region capital

• Other city

LATIUM Italian region name

Pantelleria

Mediterranean Sea

MALTA

Political Map

8°E 10°E 12°E 14°E

HOW THE GOVERNMENT WORKS

Italy is a democratic republic. There are two parliamentary chambers, the Chamber of Deputies and the Senate of the Republic, which are directly elected by the people. The president is elected not by the people but by Parliament and delegates from regional governments. The president, who serves for seven years, nominates the prime minister, who in turn appoints a council of ministers. The judiciary is independent of the executive and the legislature.

PRESIDENT OF THE REPUBLIC		
EXECUTIVE	LEGISLATIVE	JUDICIARY
PRIME MINISTER	PARLIAMENT	CONSTITUTIONAL COURT
COUNCIL OF MINISTERS	CHAMBER OF DEPUTIES 630 MEMBERS / SENATE OF THE REPUBLIC 315 MEMBERS	APPEALS COURTS

Corruption: Dirty Hands

Corruption in politics and business is an old problem, but the Italians are rooting it out. In some areas, secret criminal organizations have played a large role in society and even in local government. Gangs such as the Mafia in Sicily and the 'Ndrangheta in Calabria claim to have a code of honor, but are really just criminals. Now prosecutors are leading efforts to arrest their leaders.

In the early 1990s, the police investigated the Italian government itself. Their operation was called *Mani Pulite*, or "Clean Hands," because Italians wanted to know that their leaders were free from the "dirty hands" of corruption. Corrupt politicians and business leaders were thrown in jail. Political parties that raised money by taking bribes collapsed. They included the Christian Democracy party, which had dominated Italy since World War II.

A group of energetic new parties emerged. They included Forza Italia (Go Italy!), run by the powerful media boss Silvio Berlusconi, and the Northern League. The new parties were popular because they attacked central government. The Northern League, for example, wants northern Italy to become separate from the rest of the country. Some people fear that the Italian peninsula may once again become a jigsaw of independent states, as it was in the early 19th century.

▼ Prime Minister Silvio Berlusconi (left) and challenger Romano Prodi shake hands before their first-ever television debate during the 2006 elections.

In 2001 Berlusconi's party won elections for the second time. Berlusconi was a colorful prime minister and was highly popular among many Italians. However, he was also dogged by claims of corruption and criticism of his support for the U.S.-led occupation of Iraq.

Elections in 2006 gave a very narrow victory to Romano Prodi, leader of the Union, a coalition of parties. Prodi is often nicknamed *il Professore* (the Professor) because of his academic background. He was prime minister once before in the 1990s.

STYLE SETTERS

One of Italy's leading industries is fashion. In the 1950s Italian designers such as Nino Cerruti and Valentino led the world in creating stylish fashions. Over the next decades, Italy challenged France as the center of high-quality clothing. Armani, Versace, Gucci, and Prada became sought-after designer labels. The northern city of Milan is the center of Italian fashion. Twice a year it stages glamorous Fashion Weeks where designers show their new looks (below). The sector employs almost 600,000 people and plays a major role in Italy's exports.

An Economic Miracle

Before World War II, most Italians worked on the land, growing crops such as wheat, olives, grapes, and vegetables. After the war, the Italian government, with U.S. aid, invested heavily to create new industries or to develop existing businesses, such as textiles and automobiles.

▲ Italy's warm sunny climate is perfect for growing grapes.

In the 1960s, Italy became one of the world's leading industrial economies. Many people called its postwar recovery an "economic miracle." Italian products, such as Zanussi household appliances, Olivetti typewriters, and designer clothes, were sold

◀ Furnishings displayed in a fashionable Milan store demonstrate the style and flair typical of Italy's designers.

around the world. Sleek and sophisticated, Italian design—whether of a pair of shoes or a gleaming sports car—was widely admired and copied.

Italy's success was all the more surprising because, with the exception of natural gas, it has few natural resources. Importing raw materials, such as iron and coal, is expensive for a country's economy.

INDUSTRY & MINING

This map shows the locations of some industrial and mining operations in Italy. Most raw materials are imported.

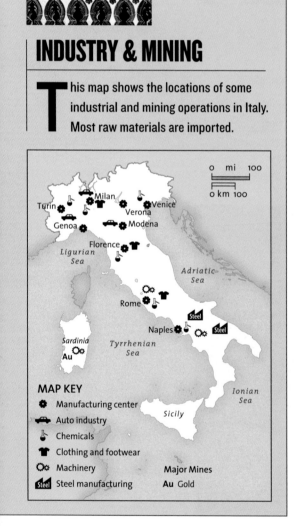

o mi 100
o km 100

Turin
Milan
Verona Venice
Genoa Modena
Florence
Ligurian Sea
Adriatic Sea
Rome
Naples Steel
Steel
Sardinia Tyrrhenian Sea
Au
Sicily
Ionian Sea

MAP KEY

- Manufacturing center
- Auto industry
- Chemicals
- Clothing and footwear
- Machinery
- Steel manufacturing

Major Mines
Au Gold

A Part of Europe

In 1957 leaders from six European countries—Italy, France, West Germany, the Netherlands, Belgium, and Luxembourg—met in Rome to sign a treaty setting up the European Economic Community (EEC). The EEC later became the European Union (EU), a group of countries that cooperate on political, social, and economic issues. In 2006 the EU had 25 members and was planning to expand further.

Italy plays a leading role in the EU. It has the fourth largest economy in the union and it is the fourth biggest contributor to its budget. Italy's commitment to Europe deepened in 2002 when the government replaced its national currency, the lira, with the euro, the new European currency.

Membership of the EU has benefited Italy in many ways. Some 59 percent of its exports are sold to EU countries—most importantly to Germany, France, and the Netherlands. The EU also invests heavily to fight poverty in regions such as Calabria and supports Italian farmers by paying them subsidies.

Businesses Big and Small

Most businesses in Italy are small or medium-size. In 2001, more than 99 percent of Italian businesses employed fewer than 50 people but about two-thirds of the national workforce. About a third produce specialized crafts, such as shoes, ceramics, and furniture. Businesses in the same region often form Industrial Districts. They work together to improve skills or to promote products abroad under the "Made in Italy" label.

There are relatively few very large companies. In 2001 just 548 companies employed a workforce of 1,000 or more. Even those firms were sometimes family owned. One of Italy's largest and

▼ A young woman crafts a violin. The first violin appeared in Italy in the 1500s, probably from the workshop of Andrea Amati in Cremona. The city later became the home of Antonio Stradivari, the most famous of violin-makers.

most famous companies, the Turin-based automobile manufacturer Fiat, is still owned by the Agnelli family, which started the business in 1899.

Many of Italy's largest concerns—including banking, textile, energy, and transportation corporations—were owned, or partly owned, by the state until the 1990s, when the government sold them into private hands.

A Leading Tourist Destination

Italy's historical monuments, artistic treasures, varied landscapes, and mild climate have long made it one of the world's top tourist destinations. In the summer months cities, such as Rome, Venice, and

▼ Villa del Balbianello's position on a wooded peninsula jutting into Lake Como and its beautiful terraced gardens make it a stop for visitors to the lakes.

Florence are so full of tourists that they feel more like open-air museums than cities. Tourism is vital to the economy. In 2004 Italy attracted 37 million visitors—amounting to almost 5 percent of global tourism—and earned 35.7 billion dollars.

Many Italians take advantage of their long vacations—four to six weeks a year—to visit resorts in their own country. In August many shops and factories close for a month and the beaches become busy. Some coastal towns make almost all of their income in August.

Italy's role as a leading tourist destination makes it one of the world's most popular and best-known nations. Italy is also politically important as a member of the powerful group of nations known as the G8, which includes the United States and Japan. Italians had to work hard to create a global economic reputation, but they have succeeded. Today, around the world, "Made in Italy" is a label that suggests stylish design inspired by centuries of artistic excellence.

▲ Urbino's dramatic hilltop position, beautiful Renaissance buildings, and art collections attract tourists year-round.

If you are assigned to write a report about Italy, you'll want to include basic information about the country, of course. The Fast Facts chart on page 8 will give you a good start. The rest of the book will give you the details you need to create a full and up-to-date paper or PowerPoint presentation. But what can you do to make your report more fun than anyone else's? If you use your imagination and dig a bit deeper into some of the topics introduced in this book, you're sure to come up with information that will make your report unique!

>Flag

Perhaps you could explain the history of Italy's flag, and the meanings of its colors and symbols. Go to **www.crwflags.com/fotw/flags** for more information.

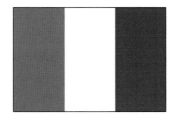

>National Anthem

How about downloading Italy's national anthem, and playing it for your class? At **www.nationalanthems.info** you'll find what you need, including the words to the anthem in Italian and English, plus sheet music for the anthem. Simply pick "I" and then "Italy" from the list on the left-hand side of the screen, and you're on your way.

>Time Difference

If you want to understand the time difference between Italy and where you are, this Web site can help: **www.worldtimeserver.com**. Just pick "Italy" from the list on the left. If you called Italy right now, would you wake whomever you are calling from their sleep?

>*Currency*

Another Web site will convert your money into euros, the currency used in Italy. You'll want to know how much money to bring if you're ever lucky enough to travel to Italy: **www.xe.com/ucc**.

>*Weather*

Why not check the current weather in Italy? It's easy—simply go to **www.weather.com** to find out if it's sunny or cloudy, warm or cold in Italy right this minute! Pick "World" from the headings at the top of the page. Then search for Italy. Click on any city you like. Be sure to click on the tabs below the weather report for Sunrise/Sunset information, Weather Watch, and Business Travel Outlook, too. Scroll down the page for the 36-hour Forecast and a satellite weather map. Compare your weather to the weather in the Italian city you chose. Is this a good season, weather-wise, for a person to travel to Italy?

>*Miscellaneous*

Still want more information? Simply go to **http://www.nationalgeographic.com/onestop**. National Geographic's One-Stop Research site will help you find maps, photos and art, articles and information, games and features that you can use to jazz up your report.

Glossary

Aqueduct an artificial channel that carries water from one location to another; it is often raised above the land like a bridge.

Bronze Age the period in human history when people learned how to alloy (mix) copper and tin to make bronze. It began between 400 and 3000 B.C. and ended when people learned how to make iron.

City-state a self-governing city that rules over the surrounding countryside.

Coalition an alliance of separate political parties with a joint purpose.

Corruption the misuse of power for private gain.

Dynasty a series of rulers from the same family.

Ecosystem a community of living things and the environment they interact with; an ecosystem includes plants, animals, soil, water, and air.

Fault line a break in the Earth's crust along which movement occurs, causing earthquakes.

Glacier a body of ice formed over thousands of years, mainly from layers of snow, that slowly flows on land.

Habitat the environment where an animal or plant lives.

Humanism an approach to life that emphasizes humanity, individualism, and the performance of public duties with the aim of improving society.

Immigration entering a foreign country with the intention of living there permanently.

Irrigate to provide with water by artificial means such as pipes, ditches, or canals.

Lava molten rock that emerges as a liquid onto the Earth's surface; also the solid rock formed when the liquid cools.

Left-wing refers to liberal or progressive political views. Left-wing parties tend to favor welfare and government intervention in the economy.

Migration the repeated, usually seasonal, travels of animals (including humans) from one place to another in search of food, better weather, and better conditions in which to raise young.

Opera a play that is almost entirely sung and which is accompanied by an orchestra.

Patriot someone who loves his or her country.

Pollution the release of harmful substances into the air, water, or soil.

Realism the faithful representation of the world in an art form such as writing, film, or painting.

Renaissance a term used to describe the period from about the mid-14th century to the mid-16th century in Europe.

Republic a government that is not ruled by a monarch. Most modern republics are led by a president or a prime minister.

Right-wing refers to conservative political views. Parties of the right tend to favor tax cuts and giving greater freedom to businesses.

Species a type of organism; animals or plants in the same species look similar and can only breed successfully among themselves.

Subsidy financial aid or support through the granting of public assistance or government bonds.

Bibliography

Blanchard, Paul. *Blue Guide to Northern Italy*. New York: W.W. Norton, 2005.

Domenico, Roy. *The Regions of Italy: A Reference Guide to History and Culture*. Westport, CT: Greenwood Press, 2002.

Duggan, Christopher. *A Concise History of Italy* (Cambridge Concise Histories, Updated Edition). Cambridge: Cambridge University Press, 1994 (reprinted 2000).

Holmes, George. *The Oxford Illustrated History of Italy*. Oxford: Oxford University Press, 2001.

http://www.britannica.com/ (*Encyclopaedia Britannica* online)

Further Information

NATIONAL GEOGRAPHIC Articles

Nature and Geography

Vidal, Gore. "Amalfi Coast." NATIONAL GEOGRAPHIC TRAVELER (October 1999): 148-150.

White, Mel. "La Dolce Vita: Italy's Lake District." NATIONAL GEOGRAPHIC TRAVELER (May/June 1997): 50–69.

Zwingle, Erla. "Po: River of Pain and Plenty." NATIONAL GEOGRAPHIC (May 2002): 92–115.

History

Bennett, Paul. "In Rome's Basement." NATIONAL GEOGRAPHIC (July 2006): 88–103.

Reid, T.R. "The Power and the Glory of the Roman Empire." NATIONAL GEOGRAPHIC (July 1997): 2–41.

Zwingle, Erla. "Italy Before the Romans." NATIONAL GEOGRAPHIC (January 2005): 52–77.

People & Culture

Carcaterra, Lorenzo. "The Real Italy." NATIONAL GEOGRAPHIC TRAVELER (November/December 2001): 38–54.

Zwingle, Erla. "Italy's Endangered Art: A Nation of Art Lovers Finds New Ways—and Will—to Save Its Priceless Legacy." NATIONAL GEOGRAPHIC (August 1999): 90–109.

Web sites to explore

More fast facts about Italy, from the CIA (Central Intelligence Agency): www.cia.gov/cia/publications/factbook/geos/it.html

The Italian Tourist Board gives information on regional travel, events, museums and other items of interest: www.italiantourism.com

Interested in soccer? Find out about the Italian team's glorious victory in the 2006 World Cup: fifaworldcup.yahoo.com

Curious about the Vatican? You can research news items about the Vatican, or the Vatican museums: www.vatican.va

Find out more about the Vatican's Swiss Guard: www.vatican.va/roman_curia/swiss_guard

Fascinated by volcanoes? You can visit Vesuvius: volcano.und.edu/vwdocs/volc_images/img_vesuvius.html

Index

Credits

Picture Credits

Front Cover—Spine: John and Lisa Merrill/Corbis; Primary: Fotostock/Alamy; Lo far left: Fabio Muzzi/www.fabiomuzzi.it; Lo left: Vittoriano Rastelli/Corbis; Lo right: Laura Ronchi/Getty Images; Lo far right: Ewing Galloway/Index Stock Imagery.

Interior—Corbis: Alinari Archives: 33 up; Bettmann: 34 up, 44 lo; Maurizio Brambatti/EPA: 51 lo; Daniel Dal Zennaro: 52 lo; Michelle Garrett: 48 lo; Dave G. Houser/Post-Houserstock: 5 up; Hulton-Deutsch Collection: 35 lo; David Lees: 15 lo; James Leynse: 22 up; Gunter Marx 22 lo; Fillippo Monteforte/EPA: 3 right, 46-47; Vittoriano Ristelli: 13 lo; Guenter Rossenbach/Zefa: 21 lo; Royalty Free: 41 lo; Studio Patellani: 45 lo; Christof Wermeter/Zefa: 21 up; Graham West/Zefa: 13 up; Getty Images: Stefano Amantini/Laura Ronchi: 20 up; NG Image Collection: 14 up; William Albert Allard 3 left, 11 lo, 36-37, 43 up, 55 lo; Ira Block: 42 up; Jodi Cobb: 43 lo; Cotton Coulson: 57 up; Macduff Everton: 56 lo; Todd Gipstein: 53 up; Anne Keiser: 2 left, 6-7; Bob Krist: 1; Luis Marden: 2-3, 24-25; Albert Moldvay: 10 up; O. Louis Mazzatenta: 26 lo; O. Louis Mazzatenta/Museo Captiolino, Rome, Italy: 29 up; Klaus Nigge: 23 up; Richard Nowitz: 28 up; Winfield Parks: 30-31; Carston Peter: 14 lo; Norbert Rosing: 18 up; Tino Soriano: 53 lo; James Stanfield: 41 up; George Steinmetz: 42 lo; Theo Westenberger: 38 up; NHPA: Maurizio Valentini: 2 right, 16-17; Nature Picture Library: Dietmar Nill: 12 lo

Text copyright © 2006 National Geographic Society
Library edition ISBN: 978-0-7922-7666-1
First paperback printing 2009
Paperback ISBN: 978-1-4263-0567-2
Published by the National Geographic Society.

For more information, please call 1-800-NGS-LINE (647-5463) or write to the following address:

NATIONAL GEOGRAPHIC SOCIETY
1145 17th Street N.W.
Washington, D.C. 20036-4688 U.S.A.

Visit the Society's Web site at www.nationalgeographic.com

Printed in United States of America

Series design by Jim Hiscott.
The body text is set in Avenir; Knockout.
The display text is set in Matrix Script.

Front Cover—Top: Girl chases pigeons in Piazza San Marco Venice; Low Far Left: Sunflowers in Tuscany; Low Left: An engineer works on a Ferrari engine at the factory in Maranello; Low Right: Temple of Castore and Polluce, Agrigento, Valle Dei Templi, Sicily; Low Far Right: Active volcano, Etna, Sicily

Page 1—View of a traditional stone farmhouse on a hillside in Tuscany; Icon image on spine, Contents page, and throughout: Moorish columns on cloister at Villa Rufolo, Ravello, in Salerno.

09/WOR/1

Produced through the worldwide resources of the National Geographic Society

John M. Fahey, Jr., *President and Chief Executive Officer*; Gilbert M. Grosvenor, *Chairman of the Board*; Nina D. Hoffman, *Executive Vice President, President of Books Publishing Group*

National Geographic Staff for this Book

Nancy Laties Feresten, *Vice President, Editor-in-Chief of Children's Books*
Bea Jackson, *Director of Design and Illustration*
Virginia Koeth, *Project Editor*
Lori Epstein, *Illustrations Editor*
Stacy Gold, *Illustrations Research Editor*
Carl Mehler, *Director of Maps*
Thomas L. Gray, *Map Editor*
Priyanka Lamichhane, *Assistant Editor*
R. Gary Colbert, *Production Director*
Lewis R. Bassford, *Production Manager*
Vincent P. Ryan, Maryclare Tracy, *Manufacturing Managers*

Brown Reference Group plc. Staff for this Book

Project Editor: Sally MacEachern
Designer: Dave Allen
Picture Manager: Becky Cox
Maps: Martin Darlinson
Artwork: Darren Awuah
Index: Kay Ollerenshaw
Senior Managing Editor: Tim Cooke
Design Manager: Sarah Williams
Children's Publisher: Anne O'Daly
Editorial Director: Lindsey Lowe

About the Author

ROBERT ANDERSON received his MA degree in European languages and literature from the University of Exeter, United Kingdom. For the last 12 years he has worked as an editor and writer of books for young readers and has taught in elementary schools in both the U.K. and France.

About the Consultants

MICHAEL DUNFORD is a professor of economic geography at the University of Sussex, United Kingdom. His research focuses on European economic, regional, and urban geography, and he has recently co-authored a book entitled *After the Three Italies* (2006). Professor Dunford is an honorary member of the Società Geografica Italiana, and has taught in and made many research visits to Italy.

DR. FRANCESCO PASTORE is an assistant professor of economics at Seconda Universita di Napoli, Italy. He is also a research fellow at IZA Bonn, Germany. Born and raised in Naples, he received his econmics and business degree from the University of Naples "Federico II." His Ph.D. in economics was awarded by the University of Sussex in 2001. Dr. Pastore's articles on regional issues in Italy and in Eastern Europe have been published in international journals and books.